To Become a Landlady

Eleanore Hill

BETA BOOKS

To Become a Landlady © 2014 Beta Books
ISBN 978-0-930012-15-1   Cover art by Stanley Trent Bemis
Beta Books is an imprint of Bandanna Books

LITERARY FICTION

The Marty Trilogy—Eleanore Hil **Aurora Leigh**, E.B. Browning **Hadji Murad**, Tolstoy **The Basement**, Newborn **The First Detective.** Poe **Matilda**, Mary Shelley

SPECULATIVE FICTION

Frankenstein, Mary Shelley   **The Martian Testament,** Newborn

HISTORY

Mitos y Leyendas/Myths and Legends of Mexico. Bilingual
Beechers Through the 19th Century   **Uncle Tom's Cabin**, Stowe

SCHOOLING

Don't Panic: Procrastinator's Guide to Writing an Effective Term Paper   **First Person Intense**   **Italian for Opera Lovers**
French for Food Lovers   **Doctorese for the imPatient**

SPRITUAL

Ghazals of Ghalib   **Gandhi on the** *Bhagavad Gita*
Gospel According to Tolstoy   **Everlasting Gospel**, William Blake

LOVE

Dante & His Circle   **Vita Nuova**   **Sappho**   **Venus & Adonis**

STAGING SHAKESPEARE

DIRECTOR'S PLAYBOOK SERIES: Hamlet   **Merchant of Venice**
Twelfth Night   **Taming of the Shrew**   **Midsummer Night's Dream**
Romeo and Juliet As You Like It Richard III Henry V Much Ado About Nothing Macbeth Othello Julius Caesar King Lear Antony and Cleopatra

7 Plays with Transgender Characters   **Falstaff: 4 Plays**

TEACHERS ONLY

(Q & A, glossaries, critical comments)

Areopagitica, John Milton   **Apology of Socrates, & Crito,** Plato
Leaves of Grass, Walt Whitman   **Sappho, The Poems**

To Become a Landlady

—a testimonial—

to countless landladies everywhere

The Landlady

To become a landlady, it usually takes going through hard times. Most landladies I know are either divorced or widowed. They are not the women who have money to invest in property and do so with the idea of renting out that spare room. No one would be a landlady if they could avoid it. Down through history, women opened their homes to boarders to get by financially after their husband left or died. Becoming a landlady is a process, never planned, and not a choice a woman would make if she could help it. It's not fun. You can make the best of it if you have a sense of humor.

The making of a landlady requires that you have a house with an extra room. This is the basic landlady position. You wouldn't have to rent out that room if you had more of a situation at your disposal, a bigger house, more money, other resources that let you go out and earn a living away from home. Maybe you combine the two, working and renting out to get by. Some people will do anything to avoid becoming a landlady: break their foot pushing the elderly in wheelchairs and going on Workman's Comp, seeking out financial help from community organizations, going without. I've seen people sell their house rather than stoop to becoming a landlady. It is a thankless position and a real inconvenience to have a stranger under your roof. It robs you of your solitude, unless you call going to your room the way you did as a kid, solitude. It pricks your ears in a way no other role does, listening for the intruder to enter your space. The car driving up, the footsteps, the snap of the door. The opening and closing of his door, the bathroom and kitchen faucets going on and off. The washing machine and dryer. Doors creaking even after you oil them. The refrigerator door poofing open and closed. You learn about your need to be alone, undisturbed. Being a landlady ruins your private life and you anguish all the way to the bank about it. It's a trade-off.

You can't go home as a landlady because your home is now a business. You are no longer just a woman but a woman who collects money from a tenant who resides under your roof. Even with references (which are easy to fake) you never know who you are going to get. The "nicest" people can turn into tenants from hell overnight (when they've given 30 day notice and want to sit on their deposit for a last month's rent, and you know they've wrecked the carpet).

Take the Woman...

Take the woman who decided to rent out that spare room. She got a call from "a nice young man." These were her words later. She said he could pay her only the rent, and from month to month. He moved in after paying the first month's rent and when the second month came around, told her he didn't have it. She didn't know what to do. It was an eye opener to her, someone simply not having a second month's rent. She believed him, though, and said that she needed the money. That didn't seem to twist his heart strings any, and he stayed in his room and ignored her. So, she went to his, which was her own, door, and knocked. She wanted to discuss it. He closed the door in her face and said he was busy. She went to her room and stared at the air in disbelief. How was it that she had a man in her house who was living there without paying her any money? She didn't know what to do.

She called a friend who called a friend who rented out rooms. The friend of a friend called her and asked her a few questions. Did she bother to get a rental agreement made out with all the stipulations for renting a room in her house? Did she have a last month's rent and a deposit of the same under her belt as a back-up? Well, all she could do then, is serve a three-day notice of Pay or Quit. What was that? You get them at any stationery store, follow the directions and serve them to the tenant. He will have seven business days to answer, and then you can file an Unlawful Detainer and when the judge rules on it, hire the marshal to serve it to the young man within another ten working days, and he will have to move out. He will not have a choice at that point.

The marshal will stand by and usher him out without any of his belongings, because, by law, he was served with the deadline for eviction, and should have already moved.

Wow! She had never heard of such tales. And she was scared. Now, where do you get the Three Day Notice to Pay or Quit? What does it look like? How do you fill it out?

What if he doesn't leave, even then? Why would he do this? It was very popular for tenants to do this five years ago before the State of California Tenant's Association in Sacramento changed the laws governing rentals.

"Professional tenants," as they were called by the court in jest, moved into a place when they found a gullible landlady (or landlord, which is rare), and simply stopped paying rent. It used to be the eviction process dragged out for three months. So, they would live free and then skip out just before the marshal came out to take them by the arm or arrest them if they refused. The landlady would lose all that rent. Now the judge requires a tenant to put up the rent each month that it takes for the eviction process, so the tenant cannot live rent-free. The court may ask you to hand over the deposit. This is a suggestion. They cannot demand it. Do not do this. It may be the only money you have to reimburse yourself with. No telling if you'll ever see it again once an attorney gets it into his or her hands to "hold" for you. The court can hold the rent a tenant hands over to pay the landlady with when the case is closed, no matter who wins. Rent is due if one is residing in a rental, unless there is neglect to make repairs if conditions are hazardous to the tenant, such as leaky roofs, rats (unless it was rat-free, and sloppy tenants created a stench that attracted them). All this has to be set before the judge, and rents due will be paid by those monies the court holds. This information is all available in the current *Landlord's Handbook*, by Brown and Warner.

There are sample copies of all official notices pertaining to tenants. Also, there is a local organization paid by tax payers called Landlord Tenant Mediation Task Force, which is helpful for working out problems with a mediator. Another organization you can become a member of and benefit from for all paperwork provided as well as an attorney who will reduce fees for members, is the local Rental Housing Association.

Whether the lawyer who works for this group is reputable or not needs to be reviewed by the state legal supervisory board. In the past, an attorney in this capacity has taken advantage of his monopoly on the market and charged more to make up for the ten percent discount he pretends to give clients in hiring him. There are, by word of mouth, excellent eviction attorneys who stick to a reasonable price, with a package that guarantees getting an undesireable tenant out. To evict a tenant yourself, the rule of thumb is to simply give a 30-day notice without stating a reason why. Reasons can create descrimination battles in court. The law is on the side of the homeowner for simply not wanting someone in your house anymore. If you say it's because they are too old, a certain ethnicity, gender, they can argue in court. The only legal reasons for eviction that you can mention is for being a "nuisance," which is the word the state manual uses for a tenant consistently late in paying the rent, or destructive to the property.

You cannot evict for retaliation. The book will give you all the rules and regulations, which are constantly being updated.

And Then There Was Mel Halderman

He fancied himself a lady's man. Or a ladies' man. At the time, I had the hairy tenant in the house, with his hairy dog and cat, who never had a date. Only after Mel moved out did I see the green-eyed monster in the hairy tenant when he said that Mel thought of himself as a "lady killer." The hairy tenant was educated, held a good job in charge of a lot of people, travelled to give talks, and would be considered a success in the world of earning a good living, yet, all along he had looked with some jealousy on this guy who lived in the studio in the back who had one woman after another crawling all over the place. One would be coming in the front door while another would be making it out the back. That wasn't the tenant who made me add the infrequent overnighters to my list of rules. That tenant would come later.

Mel rented the studio with his lady masher's charm. He had a snip of a nose, sleek dark hair oiled back in the style of Elvis just before Elvis went sideburned-out. He had blue-brown eyes, not really hazel. One day they'd be blue as the sky, the next brown.

He didn't wear colored contact lenses, as one tenant did, but she would come later, too. Mel let me believe I was renting just to him. After he moved in, a big outboard motorboat appeared parked in the easement next to the studio. This would run up the water bill in a time of drought, just to flush out the engine with the garden hose. Then a huge motorcycle with all the trimmings of silver, chrome, black leather, white leather, appeared parked behind the boat. Only much later did I discover that a huge organ had been moved into the studio, which had to be kept at a certain temperature or it could pop its strings. This was contrary to the rental agreement he signed saying he would conserve on heat, making sure everything was turned off when he left for work or travelled. I learned that the thermostat had been kept on 75 degrees.

Bills from all the department stores began coming in the mail. And bills for the boat and motorcycle. Credit card bills flourished, filling the mail box out front. One day I was invited into his domain while he fished around for his rent in one pocket after another, coming up short, saying he would give me the rest of it in two days when he got paid.

This would be an on-going plight. He would never have all the rent at one time, and he would end up moving out without paying his last month's rent, owing me a hundred dollars or so, even over what his deposit was worth. Early on, now, I glanced at his midnight blue furnishings, all bedroom pieces that were made of some shimmery plastic and stood seductively in their places just waiting for the next lady to be inserted in place. There was the luxurious bed, yet unpaid for, and the bureau with the streaks of silver like flying semen for drawer handles, the ample round mirror framed in the same midnight blue hue reflecting the roomful of sultry, wanton furnishings. And Mel, all suave and oiled, glistening like his boudoir bedroom set, smiled and smiled, promised and promised, saying he was "not that kind of guy who wouldn't pay his rent." Well, he had to believe it.

I knew that if he had to say it, he would absolutely

skip out owing me something. And I'd tried to prevent it by keeping up a dialogue with him about the balance owing. He kept up the goodwill, fooled me up to a point. As a landlady, I've never gotten used to boldfaced lying. Looking you right in the eye with such sincerity, and lying through their teeth.

Mel was a passive, sweet liar. There were even cat fights over him. A few women had the essence of a hair pulling, one not knowing about the other, one day. Mel handled it by saying his father was dying and he had to go back to Mississippi. He left all three of us standing with our mouths open. Without him, my empty palm looked ridiculous, and the two women hissing and clawing at the air lost its credibility. Mel was only a voice on the other end of the phone who sugared us with promises, saying he wasn't that kind of a guy to do what he had done.

While he was gone, he had given his key to both women. That's how they found out about the other. They had both decided to sleep in his bed, smell his aftershave on the pillow, browse through his CD and VCR collections, lounge back and daydream about his love making, on the same night. Why Mel thought this would never happen is beyond reason. He was just that kind of guy, though. He liked his women coming and going, touching his belongings, keeping up their longing, and did not have it in him to calculate that one might run into the other. Or, if he'd schemed to have them come face to face, he figured he'd convince each one that the other didn't mean a thing to him. And she believed it. I think he was just that kind of guy to believe it, too.

I finally got a call from one woman who confessed she was in love with him and would I please stop asking him for the late rent, that it made him nervous and anxious, and you know, really bothered him, and he was such a nice guy, that I should just let up, back off, and trust him. That's what she, herself had to do, she confessed, when I told her it was none of her business. She began to break down in tears and tell me that she had to just trust him, that he was not the kind of guy to cheat anybody. Yeah, yeah.

I got a locksmith and had the locks changed while he was out of town for a month, letting his rent sit on his deposit, letting his girlfriends run rampant through my property. I had other tenants to think of, their security, their privacy. It was within my right to ban all the traffic. Mel had rented the place, not the whole town. I told him this over the phone. He threatened that if I let his organ get cold, all the strings would pop and he would hold me liable for it, and that it was a very expensive instrument. I told him I couldn't have his girlfriends coming over and rummaging through the other tenants' storage. Mel's studio opened onto the large storage area that we all shared.

When Mel came home, I had a sheriff standing by to let him into his studio with my new set of keys. If he had arrived home without a way to get into his place, I would have violated his tenancy. As it was, I was simply within my rights to protect my property for the other tenant's sake. There was nothing he could complain about. He blinked a couple of big-eyed blinks, slunk around as if to sniff his organ and midnight blue unpaid for furnishing and dismissed the sheriff.

Mel moved out after that because I wouldn't let up on asking for the rent and half believing that he intended to pay it. He skipped out in the dark of night to an address unknown. I ran into him at a restaurant one night, and he ducked his oily head into his collar. He had a beautiful woman with him. They were dining on steak and the works!

In General

ABOUT SPILLS :
No tenant has ever admitted to one. You say, "What's this dark spot on the carpet?" and they look blank as if they've never even seen a floor before, cannot see the spot you're looking at, and basically don't understand what you are talking about. Even with video taping the carpet and taking snapshots to prove that the floor had no spots upon their moving in, a tenant will play innocent. Walkthroughs beforehand also fall ineffective after a move out. They'll argue that they have no idea how that spot got there, that it was not there when they cleaned, as if somehow, it seeped up from the foundation mysteriously or the quality of the carpet somehow absorbed it from the air.

The spot must always be the result of the weakness of your premises, not their fault.

ABOUT WHO YOU ARE:
You may not give a thought to your social image out there in the world, or have a very well-developed self image that you function out of, but your tenant will have you defined down to your smallest toenail. They notice everything about you, because it is as vital to their survival as to any animal who enters another's territory. The tongue may remain silent, but their eye is going in and catching snapshots of who you are, who they will be dealing with, who they are putting

themselves into close proximity with. And the eye is not kind. With one glance, that first meeting, when you introduce yourself, shake hands, their eye will take in your whole situation. As will yours theirs.

Predatory people will size you up as victim material. And victims will force you to abuse them in the end. Some of this is conscious behavior and some is not. When a landlady is a victim type, even victim type tenants may end up becoming predatory.

As much as we don't like to admit we do this, we do it. We pass judgement on one another round the clock. It's the way the mind works. You may not let it reach consciousness, lean toward your parlor manners taught you in childhood, but the eye is vulgar, a truth or fact seeker, and goes in and grabs a look and makes evaluations quicker than the mind can shift into gear. You may discover what you think later, after you have changed your social smile to a grimace in the privacy of your own room.

The mind is slower than the eye, as is evident when something comes flying through the air and you blink just in time, before you even knew what was happening. That's the motor reflex, but the optic nerve is just as quick to send a message to the brain when it sees "danger." One glance is like a photograph, and one picture is like a thousand words. If we had to rely on the spoken language to get all out messages about each other, we'd go around not knowing most things. Most of what we store inside our brains is from observation. All you have to do is watch a baby of any kind, human or puppy, kitten, bird, monkey, with a close-up lens on their eyes, to study how the eye studies all movement, shape, color, size, while the ear and nose help out on their levels. This, to assess safety. Survival is everything. And as a landlady, you are being assessed and assessing to assure your survival. Of course, no one thinks of it this way at the time; but when something goes wrong, your very immune system is a stake, which reduces down to your very life being at stake over the choices you make.

Self-definitions are avoided like the plague in public. Only in front of the mirror, do we turn sideways and flex and smile, bend in closer and examine our teeth and skin and hair, and make over ourselves like strangers who have just discovered the wonder of us. We like to defy description. Who can really describe us? Well, a social worker can, and will if there is a problem. Or a person of the law. We have a socio-economic description for sure. Our drivers' licenses describe our size, gender, and coloring and age. We are described by property ownership very definitely down at the Court House in Records. The Health Department, Fire Department, City or County Planning Departments have very rigid descriptions of you as a home owner if any questions come up about your property. The Public Utilities knows your description, too. The address is a description to the Post Office. And if you have a business license of any kind, you are described in financial terms. So, to be realistic, a landlady must know her description in relationship to those who come to rent a room from her. And this is relative. If a person of color comes knocking on your door, they will see white and you will see black first off. More information will come as you talk. Gender, age, size, interests, employment, quirks, etc. all come into play when screening a potential tenant. Too often white people show a humanitarian sentimentality attitude toward someone non-white which goes like this, " Oh, how sweet. From Korea. My father was in the Korean War. My gardener is Filipino, but I guess that isn't...

uh. Oh, my uncle was on Iwo Jima, and my brother was in Okinawa. Korean? Oh, there's a market out near the campus... I bought my grandchild one of those Chinese puzzles you can't get your fingers out of. You know? Oh, I guess that isn't Korean, but my son used to go to Hong Kong a lot..." This is either spoken or thought. And it shows.

I will say, at this point, I am a white, and my experiences as a landlady are "white," if there is such a thing. And I have been reacted to as who I am, white, older, female, alone, educated as a teacher and therapist. It shows. My eyes are blue, skin freckled, slender of body, casual of dress, usually barefooted at home where I meet and greet my potential tenants which doesn't immediately demand respect. I talk too much and reveal more than I need to which gives the air of friendliness, but once they are settled in, keep to myself and say very little in passing from that point on.

I have had tenants of all races and ethnic groups give me a hard time, but no more or less than white tenants. The only difference I noticed was that tenants of color, be it brown or black, red or yellow, pull out their color as being the reason for any problems. If a tenant can't pay the rent and are of a minority group, it's because they are of that ethnicity that I'm suddenly demanding them to pay up, for example. A landlady becomes an easy scapegoat for whatever hardship a tenant suffers. Whatever is a personal issue for a tenant, becomes their issue with the landlady. Some tenants walk around with a chip on their shoulder, and are just waiting to vent anger. What you represent as a landlady to your tenant can become a sore point at a later date. I was accused of being a homeowner by a New York Italian who was snorting his money up his nose. I told him, just before evicting him after discovering his cocaine habit, "There goes your mortgage."

The first time I ever rented out a room in my house was to a Japanese young woman. She had a last name like Jones, said her father was Caucasian, was a student who also worked part-time. I didn't like the idea of renting out a room at all, but found I had to or go get a full-time job myself. I decided I would sacrifice my privacy with a tenant. I didn't know what this meant at the time. I took her money and talked out the rules of the house. It was a verbal agreement that she was renting ONLY a room and would not have the run of the house, just kitchen privileges. One daughter was still living at home at the time, and took a dim view on the whole thing. She resented my violating the sacredness of the family home by allowing a stranger in just for money. But, I was newly divorced and NEEDED the money in order to keep my house from being sold. It seemed like good a solution to me at the time.

The girl agreed to the verbal stipulations, nodding and nodding that she was not to use the living room. She was to do her living in her room, such as read and watch T.V. So, I came home on that first day and there she was sitting in the living room watching television with my daughter. I put my groceries down in the kichen, on the counter that separated the living room from the kitchen, and pinned her with my eyes. She looked up and said "Hi," and then continued to laugh and talk and watch the tube. I was surprised. We had gone over exactly this: no living in the living room. I put my groceries away and began cooking, within full view of the living room. It was the first time I realized that my privacy had been violated. As I worked, I felt self-conscious. I didn't know that my face moved as I thought my thoughts, and cooked my meals. I went through all the evening's motions with the girl's presence within view, and I felt that I could not let down my hair, after a day out in the world where I had to watch myself. Now, I was having to watch myself right in my own house. I was enraged.

After she went to bed, I told my daughter that the girl was not suppose to be in the living room. My daughter just shrugged. She felt sorry for me. I'd brought this on myself. "She saw me sitting here, Mom, and so she joined me, that's all." I stewed over it. My daughter was family. This girl was a tenant. That was two different things. I wasn't her mother and I wouldn't have her in my living room. I knew there was a distinction between renting out a room and sharing a house. I had intentionally set a lower rent because of the restrictions, and now the tenant was getting the whole enchilada, or should I say, won ton, for the price of a side dish. In those days it was $250.00, which included all the utilities they could leave on; and they left everything on, heating blankets, heater and lights in every room with all the windows open.

I knocked on the girl's door that night and asked if she remembered what our verbal agreement was. She spewed that my daughter got to watch T.V. in the livingroom, so why couldn't she. I explained that there were two sets of rules, one for tenants and one for family. She had a tiny fit of facial expressions right there in front of me, closed the door in my face, and that was that. The next day she wasn't around. She was never around after that. I knocked on her door, tried the door handle when she never answered, and found it locked. I realized that she had moved out after several days, had locked both her hall door and the door to the outside when she left, took the key and had her revenge. I had the door taken off the hinges to enter the room, changed the locks, and after realizing the wrath of a tenant who feels wronged, decided that I needed to make keys and keep a set for myself when I rented to a new tenant. After going to all that expense, she called, apologized, wanted to return the key to get her deposit back, and I complied. I was innocent in those days, before the wear and tear of being a landlady begins to show. I still trusted people and believed them to be good human beings who, like me, really didn't want to hurt anyone. I had a lot to learn.

The next tenant was a young man with a black dog who needed a place to stay on his way up to some mountain where there were suppose to be vibrations from Indians. That should have been enough to clue me in, but I was still in a myopic state of looking right into the eyes of fellow humans and believing them to be good, and also fresh from my humanitarian upbringing. I thought in terms of "helping" people. It would take me a long time to get over that, if I ever have. It still rears its ridiculous head and gets me in trouble from time to time, dealing with strangers who need a place to lay their weary heads.

The Number One Complaint

The number one complaint of roommates I've listened to is someone in the house's inability to wipe off a countertop. This house-cleaning skill or lack of it does not belong to any one age group. It ranges across the board from young to old and men or women. I stood talking to one of my young men tenants once while he cleaned up after making pasta, a typical food they know how to cook. He had already opened the jar of sauce, put out his plate, was turning off the flame and about to pour the pasta into a colander. The countertop was spattered with water, splops of sauce, crumbs from the hunk of french bread he planned to eat with his already white flour meal, and some sprinkles of garlic salt and smears of butter. He was telling me of a recent mountain climbing excursion he'd just taken with a friend. At the time, I didn't know "mountain climbing" was a trendy sport being taken up by the youth in their early twenties. They got to order all the equipment and costuming out of these wonderful catalogues that come in the mail, and with such attire, drive in their beautiful jeep-like automobiles, and park near a popular "mountain." The mountain turned out to be a sheer slice of rock sticking up about thirty or forty feet along a popular hiking trail. It was not a long walk from the car, and the beautiful colorful clothing on the backs of these young people was just like the ad in the catalogues. They were at various points of the climb, adjusting their brand new and never-been-smudged ropes and ratches, all the stainless steel sending a star out from its sheen in the sunlight. Where had I ever come to believe a mountain climber was some rugged individual way off somewhere risking his life, tormented by citylife, and seeking a challenge. These were just boys and girls with toys.

As the young tenant told of where and when and who, not mentioning how or what, he began cleaning up after himself. It was pitiful. I saw his long delicate hands with the perfectly clean and cut nails, smearing an unsqueezed dish rag across the tile of the counter top leaving the crumbs and sauce and butter redistributed. He then dripped his way to the sink, threw the rag in, and turned to pick up his plate and eat his meal. I held my tongue. I had resolved not to be a den mother early on. I was a landlady in my home, not a teacher, mother, nurse, policewoman, or any other role. It was hard to turn my back and not rinse and squeeze out the rag, saying nicely, "Oops, you missed a spot," and wipe the countertop off the way I like it, simply wiped and clean.

It occurred to me to incorporate housecleaning skills in my screening process when interviewing possible tenants. I would ask them first if they had any. If they didn't know what I meant by "housecleaning skill," I would eliminate them right off. If they said, "Yes," I would hand them a rag and ask them to show me. If their beautiful brand new hands, supposing it is a young person looking for a room, didn't know how to hold the rag, wet the rag, squeeze the rag, and wipe with the rag, then they'd have to be eliminated. If they were able to do the first step of the skill, and then throw the rag in the sink wet, to stew and stink, they'd be eliminated. The full skill, down to rinsing out and squeezing out the rag and hanging it over the faucet to air, would get consideration.

A Night of Whiff and Wiff!

I don't even want to think about it, but here goes. She was a blonde, too fancy for my place. But, she liked it and wanted to move in immediately. She drove a vintage Mercedes and said she had been living just a couple of miles up from me, but way back around winding roads in the hills, and her car was sucking up the gas, and she was separated from her husband, working at The Girls Inc. and wanted to save money. My house was closer to the freeway and just a zip into town and she'd be there. She informed me, after she plopped an oversized divan of lime green in the middle of my livingroom (of course she asked, and I was stupid enough to say yes), that she was very sensitive to odors. She lifted her nose and moved it like a possum searching for persimmons. Sure enough, there was an odor. She said she couldn't live with that. (No, I didn't give her rent back and tell her it wasn't going to work out after all, since she had come in with her eyes and nose open and had been eager to take it.)

She just simply had nowhere else to go, and she hung her head, placed her long fingertips on her temples and exhaled through her long blonde nose. I fell for it. I told her I'd call Servicemaster out that night and get rid of any smell she could detect that no one in the household could. She immediately hugged me, said I was too good, and went away to bring another load in. Servicemaster showed up. The man got out his odor detector and went around the floor. Sure enough, the high whine sounded in one corner of the open closet area. The closet had had louvered door on hinges, but she had lifted them out of them, stood them in the hallway, and giving them the white glove treatment, showed me that the louvers had dust on them, that she couldn't breathe any dust. As the Serviceman set up his equipment and proceeded to suck any odors out of the room and the hallway, she then examined the couch cover up close, bending her lithe primadonna body down to actually sniff the cloth. She reared up with a wrinkled nose. That would have to be cleaned, too. I was already out a hundred dollars for the emergency call to Servicemaster after hours, but told her I had intended for some time (actually for some years) to reupholstery that couch, and promised I would do it right away.

She was a professional singer. She sang at any festivity and in several languages. She had an enormous wardrobe, which I saw as "sad sacks" hanging there. Her idea of fashion was like Goldie Locks'. After the carpet was sterilized, the couch reupholstered, and all her clothes hung in the closet as wide as the room, she still wrinkled her nose. There was still a smell. "Like dampness." She could not spend a night there, she was convinced, or she would get a headache. That there were spores in the air. Her allergies would act up. It'd cost her money to see a doctor.

In hindsight, I saw that she never intended to move in, just stash her stuff until another place became vacant within bicycling of her iob. The landlady back in the hills had died and her grown daughter wanted her out immediately. And so, she saw this little house, this little woman simple enough to care to please her, half afraid of the law, lest her place be considered dirty— and she'd taken full advantage. Her ex-husband's check bounced for the rent, as she knew it would. She knew, by the time I found out, she'd be long gone. I would have lost money running the ad and selecting her, and have to run the ad all over again. She didn't care. She cared about herself. I told her that she needed to pay the rent. She reluctantly did, a little conscience-stricken when I pointed out the effort I'd gone to to please her. She then sought my sympathy, telling me that she had had to put a large deposit down on the place closer to her job, and would have to come up with the rest of it when she moved in. Did she think I cared.

She came out in the middle of the night after some affair, and with a date. As soon as I saw her date, I greeted him. He was a friend of a friend of a friend. I'd met him at a party once. This caused her a momentary shiver, that perhaps I had dated him myself. It's a small town. And she was hanging on his arm like a starlet to a producer. He was a big guy, dark as a brute, but with blue eyes shining out. He'd been a deep sea diver turned businessman, and now he was really getting himself into her drama. I assumed he had no body odor of any kind, or she wouldn't have her nose practically under his arm, as they knocked and I answered, and she reluctantly handed me over the full deposit. The rent was used up for the month she'd waited. I suppose it was cheaper than putting everything in storage. And I'm sure she did the arithmetic with that couch which would have taken up a fourteen-by-fourteen space all by itself.

The deposit would be due to refund to her by law in three weeks. When I told her that, she went through her fingers to the temple stance again with the exhale as only a professional singer can do it, long and audible. I thought she'd never inhale again. I didn't care. She had held the leverage, and now I had it and aimed to keep it. But, just enough to press the issue, let her have a little of her own medicine, and put her through the sleepless trauma she'd put me through. It worked. She began calling, frantic. When would I refund her deposit. She just knew she shouldn't have paid it. Even her boyfriend told her not to give it to me (before he knew who I was) or she may have a hard time getting it back. I told her not to worry, that she would get it back, minus the month's utilities, the ten dollar penalty for her husband's check bouncing, and possibly splitting the Servicemaster's fee. At that, she yowled. No, she was not willing to pay part of his fee. I was suppose to rent out a clean room. That was my responsibility, not hers. There was a smell, and she hadn't spent one night there. Why must she be charged any utilities.

In three weeks I made out the check, deducting the utilities and the ten dollar fee. I assumed the responsibility of deodorizing the room, which no one but herself could smell. But, in the process, she kept using the word, "whiff"—inhaling, she'd say, "Oh, I can smell it with just one whiff. " I wonder if singers have extraordinary olfactory lobes.

And the cleaning man kept saying, "You won't smell nuffin' ma'am, when I get through wiff this job. I axed my boss what to use to get rid of odors, and he tole me to use this additive."

"Additive! Will there be an after smell?" And again the fingers to the temple, then the nose to the air, the tip of which seemed to have a prehensile tail to it, and the word, "Oh, I just got a whiff again." This, to his assurance that, "wiff this product there won't be no smell." The next day at a BBQ, there she was inhaling smoke and singing!

As a Landlady

As a landlady I've rented to a Siberian husky, two identical cocker spaniels, one white lab, a miniature doberman, a giant German shepherd, and a multitude of cats over the years. I've had people come looking for a room to rent with a mastiff, a full-sized parrot, a roomful of aquariums (I rented to this young man!), pet snakes, and an iguana. I finally decided no more indoor animals. I will still consider a small three-pound dog or outdoor cat. People always claim that their animal is completely passive, shows no animosity or curiosity, sits like a statue and never eats or goes to the bathroom.

    One such woman had a sweet female shepherd-type dog, very old. She said the dog just sat all day, slept in the shade and would not pay any attention to my outdoor cats. So, she moved in. I always feed my cats outside the kitchen door, which is on the north side of the house and fenced off from the west side yard. I laughed that every dog I'd ever had there liked to come eat the cats' food. She shook her head that her dog would never be interested at all, that the old thing was so out of it and lazy that it wouldn't be a problem. The first day she went off to work, I saw her dog lie on its belly and squeeze and contort itself to get under the gate and go sniff around the cats' dishes. I had to laugh. It also woke up to the fact of being surrounded by cats and decided to ward them all off. While she was away, that dog became razor sharp about everything around the place, discovering all the new smells, animals, food supplies, and never EVER slept, much less lazied in the shade. I became good friends with the critter. I always like to see an animal in touch with its senses, so did not mind having it sharpen them on my premises. And, I learned that it was always that way. A tenant believed one thing about their pet, and perhaps knew nothing of its other side. They may have lived in a much more sterile environment than my organic property. I found it hard to believe that they would lie. Or, when they were home, the pet simply hung around them.

The aquarium owner (whose profession was setting up aquariums) had a big dog, a mutt mix. He swore his dog would be happy in the far back portion of my long half-acre yard. It had a wormword fence with those knot holes you can see through if you put your eye right up to it. That big dog was not happy way in the back. A dog's natural place is up front where it takes it upon itself to be the guard of the territory. After marking it off with its smell, it likes to sit in the driveway and keep any intruders away. This dog's eye was always in the knot holes, and its claws tearing at the wormwood. In an afternoon, it had pulled the planks from the fence and sat in the driveway up front waiting for its master to come home from work. The master acted surprised, said his dog had never done that before. No doubt! Had he ever stashed it in a backyard before? The big German shepherd was not suppose to be able to jump a six-foot fence nor even be motivated to do so. Right! That tenant went off to work and when he came home there was his dog lolling on the driveway waiting for him, after cruising through the neighborhood, toppling over all the garbage cans and chasing cats. This particular dog, big as he was, was given to private terrors and would claw open the sliding screen and hide in the hallways inside the house on a bright sunny day. We suspected it was prompted by seeing the Dog Pound truck drive by, but could never be sure. His master said he'd found the dog years before on the street as a stray. No telling what traumas he went through that still haunted him to hide and quiver inside the dark hallway from time to time.

At one point I allowed a woman with a white lab and a man with two cocker spaniels to rent at the same time. The front yard was the one securely fenced portion of the property. These two tenants would fight over whose dog-poos were whose and refuse to pick up poops, claiming they were not theirs. It became intolerable to me who was set up to mediate. I proposed that they pick up a number of poops a day no matter what. In time, and not soon enough, each gave notice and sought other housing.

Cat owners always claim that their cat will come into the house only at night to sleep with them. And I used to believe this. Because some tenants are allergic to cats, I thought I had a hard and fast rule: No cats in the house except in your own room at night. I would come in from my back studio and find cat fur on all the chairs and couch cushions. I would see the cat following the tenant into the kitchen in the evening and sitting there watching her cook dinner. When I reminded the tenant of the rule, she would say that this is the first time this happened. After being in the classroom all day listening to school children stare you in the eye and deny the truth after being caught red-handed, it was too much. I learned from these tenants and finally refused to rent to people with pets. They ALWAYS did as they pleased and told you anything you wanted to hear. And, the pet smells ALWAYS had to be gotten rid of in a semi-expensive way, with Service Master coming out and deodorizing and using the scent detector to find the spots that needed to be shampooed.

If the cat spray went into the carpet through the pad and into a wood or concrete floor beneath, the whole carpet has to be pulled up, discarded, the floor sealed with a special sealant, and then new carpet installed. Cat smells permeate a material and cannot be cleaned most of the time. And all cats spray when other cats are on a property. Most people claim that their cat "never sprays." Male or female, a non-spraying cat will be stimulated to spray its scent on its new territory if other cats are present. It's the way they draw their boundaries. And, pet owners lie. It's that simple. Unless they have a stuffed animal, the creature is going to cause some kind of destruction while it lives at your place. And there is no realistic deposit that can cover that amount, even if it were predictable. Who is going to pay two thousand dollars to replace your carpet? What tenant will admit that his cat or dog caused the smell? They will most likely say the smell was already there, somehow, from the last tenant, even though you present them with the evidence of Service Master's services that made the room odorless. It's your word against the tenants, and the judge will yawn and ask for proof. Who can prove that the cat sprayed? Who can prove that it didn't? And who wants to go to court anyway? So, most sensible landladies will not rent to dogs and cats, birds or fish, or even bearded people who resemble beasts!

That brings me to the topic of hairy people. People with lots of long hair are a hazard to the bathroom plumbing! And people who drink are hazardous to the toilet plumbing, lurching around knocking things into it and flushing them down the pipes and not remembering that they did it, saying your plumbing is old. Only when the plumber finds their hairbrush in the pipe, does the tenant have to pay the bill and admit it isn't the plumbing. But, that's another chapter…

A Word About Hair

And then there was the college graduate with a good white collar job working with ethnics. The first thing he told me when he came to see the place was not to think anything of his long hair. That he was past his loud music and partying days, that it didn't mean he did drugs. He convinced me just by mentioning it. I figured if he was out in the open about his long hair even before I thought anything of it, he'd be okay. And he was, EXCEPT for the long hairs caught in the bathroom drains. Not only did he have long hair, but he brought a very large German Shepherd mix dog with a coat as thick as three dogs in one, and a fat cat. The cat, he brushed daily. You could tell by the coat that glistened like the pelt of a muskrat. I never thought where he might put the cat fur from the cat brush, nor gave one consideration to the amount of shedding his dog would do in the hot season. The feeble verbal agreement was that he was to sweep up any fur from around the yard. I didn't mention the floating fur that would stick to the fence, screens on the windows and sliding glass doors, or clog up the rain drains. I liked dogs in those days and just wanted it to be happy in its new environment along with the tenant.

    This tall tenant squeezed into the smallest room with visiting privileges for his dog and cat. I can't believe I allowed them in the house now that I think back. And they were in dog heaven. The three of them, hairy as they were, began to shed something fierce, and as a result I would get a knock on my door that the bathtub drain was clogged. I'd pull out the drain strainer, and obviously there would be a wad of his hair like rope causing the plug. Why he didn't put two and two, or should I say one and two together and decide that the three of them were the culprits, I'll never know. Tenants are like no other people anywhere. As soon as a normal human being with all the intelligence they made A's with, step into the role of tenant, something happens to the brain, both the tenant's and the landlady's. Both IQs drop sixty points, and the tenant goes around as if he just washed his hands and can't do a thing with them, like the hair ads used to say. Logic escapes even the ones with the PhDs. In fact, the common laborers have proved more useful when it comes to wiggling the handle of a singing toilet, or taking the garbage out.

The maintenance of the long ponytail and his dog's bath with the garden hose after a swim in the ocean, the brushing with the wire brush of them as well as his own head, my place could have passed for a grooming parlor at one glance. I didn't feel up to saying anything about all the hair. In those days, and even now, I didn't like riding my tenants. I wanted them to be mature and responsible enough to notice when their habits created destruction to the property, but the eye is blind when the place isn't theirs.

He went off, got married and bought a place of his own. I've never seen it, but I'll bet there isn't a hair in sight. I'll bet it looks like the Pound after a good hosing. I'll bet his bathroom drains are whistle clean. All it takes is one bill from the plumber or a clogged lawnmower engine from impacted fur from shedding all over the yard, to teach a lesson. It always boils down to money. Once a tenant has to part with a cent to fix a thing he's broken or ruined of his own, he'll become anal retentive; but never on your property, because, I've figured out, he wants to get his money's worth and make you spend for repairs. He likes the fact that you have to put his rent money back into making the place nice for him. The deposit is another thing. He'll fight to the death for deducting even twenty dollars if he's convinced he's done nothing wrong. The fact that this tenant's fat cat clawed a hole in the new carpet by the opening of the door, trying to dig its way under to get in or out, seemed so logical to the tenant, that the frayed strands of carpet made sense and even looked kind of nice. It was his cat. His cat could do no wrong. He even smiled, and I'm sure, laughed out loud when I left. The idiosyncracies of this tenant's cat and dog were dear to him. He was getting up there toward parenting years, and this was family. I was only the landlady. It was only my house. What about the feelings and personalities of his pets? Of course they came first.

His dog was given to bouts of hot flashes during certain times of the year and of the day. To cool off, he'd revert to type and dig a nice deep cool hole in the flower beds and under the hedgerows. I'd come upon a calla lily root-up kicked off across the lawn. Well, there goes another one, I'd think; but what of the dog's feelings? What was another hole in my great big yard? What was a yard for, anyway? I could see it in his master's eyes. I can't believe that I stood there and laughed at the antics of this dog, changing spots, digging yet another hole, not satisfied with the last one. Before that dog moved out, three years later, the wooden trim around the walkways was dug out and tossed aside. I kept fitting it back into its groove in front of the tenant to hint that he needed to mention that he would repair it by replacing it and being responsible for keeping an eye on his dog to prevent more wear and tear. But, it wasn't to be.

There was a certain kick this tenant got out of his dog's destructive behavior. The early mornings saw the dog carrying home brown paper bags of the neighbors' garbage and strewing it up and down the street. On the way to work, driving through the neighborhood and seeing garbage cans turned upsidedown and knowing his dog had raided them before the sun came up, gave this tenant a private chuckle. He was from the days of the hippy, whose dogs ran loose and pissed and pooped on the lawns of The Establishment. It was a kind of statement they laughed about in the secrecy of their communes at night. They loved to see the mayor do the splits in dog doo on the sidewalk outside City Hall. So, even with a college degree on his wall, this tenant allowed his dog to "break all the rules. " It was only when he had to buy his dog back from the Pound that he began to restrain him, with a lot of criticism for the bureucrats.

This dog seemed to sense that his lawlessness was a point of pride with his owner. He held his tail high and his tongue lollying out in a big toothy smile after each escapade as his owner mock-scolded him. He had found the dog in a desert town, lived with him near the college campus, and told of how his dog could recognize the dogcatcher's truck, and was smart enough to hide. That hiding from the dogcatcher cost me my sliding screen door. With one great paw and claw, he entered the house to hide in the hallway, shivering and shaking as if remembering the days when he was a stray. Again, the tenant saw the torn screen as a sign of his dog's spirit and IQ.

The Next Nightmare

The next nightmare of a tenant was a young man. He was in his late thirties, proud of his income as a ramp loader for an industrial corporation. He could prove by his stubs that he could afford the four hundred dollar a month rent. And he had the deposit of the same. Like a preschooler, he handed over his achievement with beaming eyes. He was an earner, a worker, a "nice" guy. I should have detected the amount of falsetto in his voice. A voice projected as if though a megaphone, or perhaps it was a voice of a ventriloquist. When he sat down for the screening interview, this big important voice began filling the room. He put on a great presentation. It impressed me. His breath smelled of cigarets, coffee, and rot, but he swore he didn't smoke. I didn't see the twitch in his eyelid until a month later when he was late with the rent. He turned out to terrorize the other tenants with his change of personality from day to day; One day, even one hour, he would be so amiable, they'd fall under his spell, the way I did during our interview. And then, snap, they'd pass him, say hi, and be met with an icy silence. He was a "neat freak" to boot. He claimed he was a vet from Viet Nam, but when I called his father toward the last, who was at Vandenberg Air Force Base, the old guy chuckled.

No, his son was never in the military, but had always liked everything neat, and would go into rages over anybody else's messes. Oh, well. Here was a tenant who couldn't stand living with people, yet couldn't afford a place alone. I had to serve him with a 30-day notice on behalf of the other tenants. He had left a row of bullets out in the hallway nook, evenly spaced, as some kind of message. I even called the police on this tenant one afternoon near the end, when he told me that if his expensive cue stick, which was a rare collector's item was ever stolen from his room, that I'd be sorry. I didn't like the tone of threat in his voice, the bullets, the way he pulled out the cue stick as leverage over me just because he was behind in his rent. I raised my voice to match his and then the police came. I lived in the back. They came around to talk and ended up telling me there was nothing they could do; that, as a tenant he had the right to yell and say just about anything, and as long as I was collecting rent, I just had to let him. They mainly scolded me, the landlady and took the tenant's side. I found that that happened any time I said, "Landlady" to an organization.

And Then There Was Buster Howard

Howard came to the interview saying he was disabled. That he had a brain injury from a fall. His little female miniature doberman pissed on my floor as he talked in his grave slow manner. I jumped up and cried out. He was shaky and apologetic. I grabbed a towel and sopped up the spot. He really wanted the room in the house and told me his dog was nervous in a new place and never did that when she felt secure. I watched the snippy little bitch snoot around rousting out the cats from every crevice where they had taken to hiding when Howard and his dog entered. She was anything but a nervous little critter. She made herself at home and was already marking her territory even as a female. Howard continued to drone on and on about his sad predicament and that he had once owned his own home and knew how to take care of the place. I pictured his carpet full of urine stains. Nevertheless, he seemed the best of the prospects and I was tired of running the ad and interviewing people. That process takes a lot out of even the best landed people. There is no way to know if a tenant is the right one, if it will go well, or if this person will turn out to be a tenant from Hell.

And, so he moved in. He said most of his stuff was in storage. He brought only enough to set up a room. He was a tall, bony man, in silk shirts and slacks. Looking at his wardrobe, as he strode around on my property made me wonder why he was so down on his luck as to have to rent a room from me, just a little woman who owned a small house out in a nowhere neighborhood. But, I put it out of my mind. I passed it off as a head injury. I wondered over what kind of fall could make you disabled. I pictured him keeling off a cliff and hitting a granite rock after the rains soften the bluffs each year. But, not in those silk shirts. He wasn't the type to hide. After giving him a receipt for the rent, I got back to my real life, and never gave him another thought. As a landlady, I do that. I try not to think of even the existence of a tenant on the premises. I have never gotten used to strangers in my territory, and so have a capacity to pretend they aren't there, unless they bring my attention to it.

Howard moved in just at the time I was having the front of the house taken out and French doors put in all across. There were forty-five feet of these bright and pretty doors put in to open up the place and let in the light. The carpenter doing the work looked up one day and saw Howard streak by with his head down, making his way to his car in the driveway. After Howard left, he asked me what Howard was doing in my house. I told him he was renting a room. The carpenter whistled quietly through his teeth shaking his head back and forth very slowly, eyes rounded in disbelief. He told me Howard had been a multimillionaire, that he and his brother had invested in some property and lost all their money, and he'd heard Howard had tried to commit suicide by shooting himself in the head. He evidently missed his brain and survived, the guy said. The carpenter went on to describe the estate Howard had owned over in Hope Ranch. He said it had a swimming pool so big it reached from here to there, all tiled in blue and white with tile spelling out the name of his girlfriend on the bottom in huge letters. Now, he knew what had become of Howard. He'd always wondered. He'd done a lot of work for him over the years.

After that, I looked at Howard differently. A tragic figure, he'd become by my carpenter's description. Howard made sure never to run into the carpenter face to face. He avoided him with an uncanny awareness where this being from his magnificent past would be. The carpenter continued to come up with tidbits about Howard. He said he'd been into drugs big time. That he had grown sons and a younger brother who had also joined Howard in having big drug parties.

The sink got clogged up while Howard lived under my roof. I clearly spelled out the conditions under which the plumbing was my responsibility. If it was faulty pipes I would fix it, but if it was misuse, such as pouring grease down the sink, the tenants would have to share the expense and call a plumber. They made a feeble attempt to remedy the situation, all in vain, still looking to me as their keeper. It was my house, after all. I had come upon the sink many times with the strainers taken out of the drain and placed up on the sinkboard, so that all the garbage off of plates went down to clog the drain. I had found grease from frying pans floating on top of the cold clogged water. I told them to call a plumber and split the cost. Howard came storming out to demand that I unclog the sink, threatening that he would have to call the Health Department if I didn't take action. He was no longer disabled, had seemed to regain his confidence on my property, over me, only a small woman of no stature, and he swelled into his old arrogant rich man selfhood before my eyes. He was, indeed, an intimidating figure. I cringed inside and coldly dialed a plumber. It was three A.M. before the plumber could come out. It fell under the category of Emergency Hours. He was a young man and very competent and honest and reasonable. I stood, seething over Howard's demands, had the sink fixed, paid the plumber, and passed the cost onto my tenants, taking Howard's from his deposit after he moved out, since he refused to share the cost at the time.

I saw Howard and his pissing doberman at a coffeeshop a few months later. He had been to his son's funeral. A forty-year-old died of an overdose. Howard was going to AA. He wouldn't speak to me. I think he knew that I had been told by the carpenter who he was. He wanted to get away from any eyes that knew him, or knew of him. He stood in line to get his specialty gourmet coffee, towering above me, turning his head the way he had to avoid the carpenter.

Before he had moved out, however, he'd come to me and apologized for lowering the boom on me. Just that gesture alone let me know that he still felt he was in the old male power role. I shrugged it off, eager for him to be gone. During his stay we had sat a spell and talked about his life. I'd listened and he told me that he had been rehabilitated from drugs and drinking. That, until he went to AA, he had never known how to express his feelings. That he'd been mean, a tyrant. Nothing about his losing money, property, trying to commit suicide. He wanted to coach my "handling property."

I was glad to see him go and take that vicious little beast of a miniature doberman with him. He truely loved the spidery creature, and the creature climbed him like a cragly old hill, simpering as if it was helpless. It was an hysterical little barker, and Howard, it turned out was a big barker, in spite of everything, when he wanted to control things.

THE THREE BIG WOMEN:

The three big women came to me during the rainy season as if somehow that had something to do with it, like giant rodents washed out of their holes. They each answered my ad for a room at different times for different rooms but all for the same reason At the time it didn't occur to me that they had been evicted and because they were undesirables They gave their references and I followed up for what good that did. They can put down anyone to say something nice about them at the end of a telephone line. And, a landlady trying to get rid of a bad tenant is unlikely to tell you how bad the tenant can be. If they don't find another place to live she's stuck with them until they do so. Even in these three cases these women got good references. And they had good jobs, except the one who was on Workman's Compensation. But I'll get to her. Here they are, one at a time

The Would-Be Carol Channing and Gidget

Carol got washed out of her live-in situation in a downpour. I returned her call on my answering machine and her mellow older woman's voice convinced me that she'd only stay at my place for a month or so, just to give her time to find another place, that she could no longer stay where she was, that it was an emergency. And, she had a teenage daughter. They were in a tight situation and wouldn't I just give them a chance to have shelter until the weather broke and she could get around and find a larger living situation. The room for rent at that moment was the smallest bedroom in the house that opened onto the deck with its own entrance. I should have been warned when she exclaimed over the "private entrance" part of the ad in the newspaper. But, my heart was intact instead of my head, and I was still a do-gooder instead of a business woman. The two can't mix if you want to avoid trouble. Poor saps can spot you miles away and tell by the intonation in your voice if you'll be a pushover or not. The slightest compassion is a dead give away.

And so Carol and her daughter, a most beautiful girl of fifteen, arrived all soaked to the bone. Carol's bones were hidden deep under a layer of flesh so thick she could pass for a budding Samurai wrestler. She was maybe five-nine in her stockinged feet, while her daughter was a mere slip of a thing with naturally blonde curly hair, blue eyes and a peaches and cream complexion. She could have been in a Malibu Beach film. She huddled next to her mother on the couch as we talked about rules of the household. I told her I was making an exception allowing two in a room and one a child on top of it. I explained that I was doing it because they had promised it would be temporary, that the girl would not bring home friends from high school to fill up the house with noise, and that it was an adult household, not geared for parties, loud music or constant company. The young girl and her mother nodded and nodded.

They brought in a truckload of stuff the first day the rain stopped. The room was stacked with packing boxes and garbage bags full of clothes and shoes. They both, as blondes, wore pink, lavender, or turquoise. When I commented on the girl's beauty once, Carol quickly said that she had looked exactly like that as a teenager herself. Well, the abundance of flesh had buried any resemblance, but I could see the coloring was similar, with a little help from Clairol on the mother's part.

It turned out Carol had a favorite glass of handblown turquoise glass which she filled regularly with wine. Those treks from her far end room to the refrigerator were frequent and grew unsteadier as the day grew longer. By night time she was doing a poor imitation of a drunk but unfortunately she wasn't acting. The beautiful turquoise glass, a large size, was never without white wine, the cocktail of the California woman. The private entrance it turned out was never without men, either for the mother or for the daughter. The only giveaway was the odd car parked down the block at the wee hours of the morning

I realized the mistake I'd made, of course too late. They were in and they were slobs. Their beds were never made, which was none of my business but the few times I delivered their mail to their open bedroom door and got a peek I was appalled. The wrinkled and soiled beds side by side along opposite walls of this narrow room were the least of it The dirty clothes were knee deep on the floor At least my carpet would be protected, I thought. But I would learn that even through all the garments old Carol could wreak havoc.

The one convincing note in Carol's plea to move in was that she was a live-in housekeeper for the elderly. There were a series of little cottages that had been revovated to look like storybook houses out of Little Red Riding Hood, which housed ninety-year-old teachers, librarians, musicians, lawyers, nurses. What becomes of these once professionals? Someone spiffs up an old house, gets licensed by the State and hires a drifter like Carol to cook and clean for these poor souls. By the look of the room she lived in now and the condition of the kitchen after she spattered it with grease from cooking, I could see why they cut her employment off. But when I'd called her job reference, the woman said she was working there. They paid two thousand a month and she could certainly afford the four hundred rent, the four hundred deposit and the fifty dollar utility bill each month. She didn't tell me that she would soon let her go because she drinks a lot like Bo Jangles and couldn t keep house if her life depended on it, which it did in fact.

Carol had no intention of looking for another place to live. She settled into her cloth nest like a fat mouse. She didn't have a hostile bone in her body and was all smiles and mellow voiced at any hour of the twenty-four that you might come across her strolling to the fridge with that bight turquoise stemmed glass in her pink day outfits or softer looser nightgowns.

She was a mod woman, still dressing like her daughter and always eager to gab. She told me she had left a young boyfriend behind in Tennessee who played guitar for the Grand Ole Opry. That she ran away from him and came out to California to be an actress, had already joined up with the Little Theater in town and was trying out for a musical with Rodgers and Hammerstein. She took her daughter to a Hollywood star hunt at the Red Lion, and the poor girl lost. I was even in disbelief. Who could have been prettier, even in a classical beauty way. She was "eye candy," as one photographer called the object of a photo that you just love to look at. Even my eye would get caught up in the dippity-do curlicues of her bone structure and the perfection of the sculpturing Mother Nature must have had fun doing on her. It looked so easy to be beautiful, so exquisitely simple, when the job is done right. But, what was missing that the talent scouts from Hollywood rejected? They came home in a bustle of pinks, turquoises, and lavenders, Carol all flushed from rubbing elbows with Hollywood and high-heeled out, while Sheba wore the big thick socks and boots of her peer group, which made her look vulnerable, given the skimpy little skirt of cotton blowing in the wind, and a half bodice that barely covered her titties. The girl was a mere beach nymph, something out of Gidget, while the mother was a whale's tail, a whopper, a big old version of what the daughter would become. And it would happen too soon.

So, they went from bad to worse living in that little room, the girl creeping around so not to get her mother evicted again. Her bellybutton always visible, and some lout hanging around in his car in front of the house on the street. Any cop could see they would be a candidate for drugs. Stupid me, I didn't have an eye for such a thing, incredible as it sounds. My eye had been adjusted long ago to the sleeze look among the young. What did I know.

Soon, letters began coming from the high school addressed to the mother of Sheba. Carol would scoff at the school's concern for her daughter's welfare, her truancy, her D average. She would tell how old her daughter was, not in years, but in sophistication. She said her daughter could handle anything and would be alright. I called Carol's other daughter and told of my concern, again being unbusinesslike. My weakness, like my mother before me, when it had been a strength in her generation, was to get involved in my tenant's lives. The older sister said that her mother was the very problem, unwilling to take responsibility for her twins, that Sheba had a twin brother who lived in L.A. and was doing fine. She had given Sheba back to Carol, trying to make her mother stop drinking and take a mother's role and give Sheba the guidance she needed just as she was venturing out as a teenager. Carol was not up to that job. She herself was coming home from the beach, tracking sand into the house, beaming over her delicious swim with a young man she was trying to pick up. Her hefty gams were rosy with the sting of the icy sea water as she made her way to the refrigerator with her turquoise glass.

Carol and Sheba both filled up the recycling bins with the giant-sized plastic empty bottles of Coke, Pepsi, some in diet and some in full sugar. A few hard liquor bottles began to appear when Carol's ex-husband, the father of Sheba, began to appear on weekends. And beer cans and bottles spilled over the bins when the boyfriend stayed over. I wondered if Carol lay there in her bed and listened to her daughter and the boyfriend in the other bed, and vice versa.

This "sophistication" talk was getting on my nerves. Carol had a birthday one weekend and wouldn't tell anyone the year she was born so that another tenant could calculate her sign under the Chinese astrological signs. Her ex came up and the boyfriend came over. They all had their heads in the refrigerator pouring and popping pop caps, fizzing in the air, glazing in the eyes, and a lot of out-of-control giggling. Everyone was having a good time, and I was the fool, they thought, who couldn't recognize hard drugs in their behavior. What was a landlady to do. I just went away, disgusted with myself for having let her tenancy come to this.

The finale came when Carol missed her old boyfriend, the young guitarist back in Tennessee, and said she was flying back, and would leave Sheba, who had now turned sixteen under my roof with her boyfriend, who was twenty-one. That's when I put my foot down. This was against the law. He was an adult, she a minor, and I was not to be harboring them in my home. Carol just laughed, saying Sheba was no minor in her experience. I held to my legality and said she would have to find them another place. The boyfriend came to the rescue and let her move in with him. Carol left, leaving a heap of garbage bags full of clothes in the closets. I took them out to the shed in the back to store them. She also left the dresser in the middle of the room.

When I moved it back I found fourteen iron burns in the carpet. Her note to me in exiting was that she just left the dresser there, that she wasn't trying to hide anything.

How transparent and childish could she get. I kept her deposit to replace the carpet. It was an industrial carpet and melted like any plastic material when burned. There were also multiple burn holes from whatever they were smoking. Smoking was not allowed in the house. They must have had an air filter to suck it up so that I never detected it.

Carol got a lawyer. I told the lawyer that I'd be eager to go to court with my photographs of the burn marks, the estimate for Carpeteria to replace the carpet, and the Servicemaster's bill for deodorizing the room from the smell of rancid smoke, etc. The lawyer must have discouraged Carol, because she dropped the case.

The sad ending is Sheba. I saw her stoned out of her mind, talking to herself, walking in dirty clothes, as if she'd slept in them, bulging at the seams like her mother. I had to look twice. What had become of the beauty just a year and a half later. Drugs, sex, rock 'n roll had evidently taken over. She was yelling at a cop in the mall and being taken into custody, the second time I saw her. She didn't recognize me. She didn't know who, where, or what was what.

I've seen Carol around town. She still strolls up and down in her pale pastel cottons, all blonded out, heftier than ever, vacant-eyed, never recognizing me either on purpose. The issue of not refunding her deposit will always be between us. She will believe that the four hundred dollars would have saved her daughter from a fate worse than death, in her mind.

But, that is the plight of the landlady. You can't save people by offering them housing. They, in fact, can wreck your place like any stray animal, kicking off dander, biting the hand that tries to help it, and go on to the next place creating the same foul smell.

Looking back, I can see exactly how I got into the Carol situation. I let her pull me in using her daughter as bait. The child needs a place off the street. Well, it didn't work. The girl is on the street big time now. All the housing in the world wouldn't have saved her. My eviction notice, the non-refunded deposit wouldn't have saved her. Carol was the only one who could have done the job; but she was having too much fun trying to be her daughter. There was a letter from Carol's mother telling her so, too. I found it in the garbage when the wind blew the lid off and all the papers around the driveway.

Goldilocks and Her Many Bearers

Goldie only dated men of color. She refused to call them Afro-Americans. She herself was a very large natural blonde with a face as pretty as a movie star. A whole trek of black men moved her in while I was out of town. I had a call from a friend about it. He was alarmed. It was a red-neck, blue-collar neighborhood, and I had no idea she was divorcing a man of color. A certain "Doc" was all she had mentioned as her friend who would move her in on a certain date. I had collected her first, last, and deposit and then had to travel. She'd told me that she was temporarily on disability insurance due to having her gall bladder taken out, and would convalesce for about three months. She liked the place because it was quiet. She was getting divorced because her husband had ordered her out of the house. And she had a cat. All of this was disclosed during the initial interview. She was a born again Christian.. That was okay with me. She attended a certain church that had a large black congregation. The members were the ones who carried her belongings into the small room to help her make the move, like a safari assisting a great white into new territory. Or worker ants transporting the big queen.

Her move-in passed without mishap and her friends never appeared again. She settled into her room with house privileges quietly with her cat. Her cat was to be restricted to the room, not to enter the house proper.

She nodded and nodded to this and thought I would never know. Evidence of cat dander began showing up on the couch and all the chairs soon. As a tenant, she tested the waters. If I didn't say anything, then the cat would soon have the run of the house. I vacuumed up the cat fur for the sake of the other tenants and did not want to create ill will by bringing it to Goldie's attention. I'm that way. I let a tenant push the rule a little before I step in, just to sidestep any confrontation. I hope for their decency. But I always find that a tenant is like a child or an animal or a rude guest. They will always try to get more than they are allowed, and they will always try to test your will against theirs. When I finally pointed out to Goldie to look directly at the cat fur on the furniture, and worse, the teething and clawing at the wicker, where bits of the splinters lay on the rug, she flatly denied that it was her cat, pointing out that there were two outdoor cats of mine, and they must have been let in, in fact, she saw them indoors once. I thought that took care of it. At least, even if she wanted to blame my outdoor cats who were so fearful of coming indoors after years of living in the yard, that they would climb the walls and yowl to get out, she knew I was aware of cats being in the living room. I still saw the fur, vacuumed it up intermittently, and again, hoped she would keep her cat in her room. She never did.

    I don't like tenants to tell on one another. It's unethical for one, and for another, sets me up as a spy, which makes the whole atmosphere unsavory. So, I kept my mouth shut and my eyes open, and I saw the cat in the kitchen one evening, sitting at the dining room table watching Goldie cook, as comfortable and fearless as if it always sat there. I came in to get my mail and pointed out the cat at the table. She gave a double take look, like, "What?" and shrugged it away, saying, "This is the first time. It followed me and I couldn't catch it." Yeah, yeah. She picked up the cat, and with an audible impatient sigh for me, carried it back to the room, this time closing her door. Her cat became a bone of contention between us. It was a cute short-bodied fluffy cat with a great big intelligent head. A sort of Ted Koppel look to it, with round eyes right in the front. I could see that the cat was Goldie's man. He strutted around her as if she was his wife. He had his way with her and she could not refuse him her company, even to go to the kitchen to cook. The way he waited at the table was very husbandlike, in the old tradition. She slaved over the hot stove while he simply waited, patient.

A bird began going crazy over its territory in the front yard. She moved in in winter, and the cat began taking over the front yard as well as the house. Each year a mockingbird nested in the overgrown pittosporum hedge. It dive bombed my cats, who ran and hid. But not Goldie's cat. The male that he was with her blessing filled him with territorial pride. Like an Aesop Fable animal, he posed on the fence post, head down, tail up in the air, waving it back and forth to entice the bird. The bird would dive and peck at this strange snaky thing in the air without a cat seeming to be attached to it, get reckless and curious, and come in too close. Surprise! The cat would suddenly rear up and strike out with lightning speed. The bird escaped her cat for weeks, while she stood in the window saying that she hoped he would get that bird for the chances it took. She accepted her cat's tactics as brilliant and said the bird deserved to die. I believed the bird would win. But she got her wish, cheering her cat on. After awhile a little pile of grey feathers on the ground by the post was all that was left. I said, "Poor bird." She laughed. "Dumb bird, you mean." She must have thought the same thing of me. I was also trying to protect my territory and was no match for the determined and tricky Goldie. The only consolation of a tenant out-smarting you, is that they lose in the end. It's your place and they have to move on eventually, no matter what they get away with while there.

Goldie went off disability compensation after three months and began working. She worked in an office somewhere, and was soon late with her rent. I had banking to do one morning, and knocked on her door. Her rent was a week late and she had not said a word to me. I had a 1% late fee which I had never applied before, trying to be the nice guy. She knew this. I knocked again. She suddenly tore the door open after a long silence, spewed into my face that I had disturbed her prayer session. I told her that I was there to collect the rent, and she did the audible sigh again, seethed in my face that she would pay it when she got her check and she didn't know when, maybe in a few days. I told her I would have to charge her a late fee because I would be charged late fees on my bills. Again she flew at me with her head forward and arms back, face frothing and said she was not about to pay for any of my late fees because of my inability to handle my bills. That was not her responsibility, that I had disturbed her prayer, that she had to pray so many minutes a day, and what was I doing coming to her door asking for the rent anyway. She closed the door in my face.

I felt my adrenalin rise. As a landlady, I knew all I had to do was bide my time, and she'd be out. There was no way she could win the big picture. In this way, I went back to my room and tried not to stew. Which is hard to do. Even when a stranger comes careening around and gets in your face with aggression, it is not easy to walk away without wanting to tear hair. I ignored her hard in passing for the next few times until she felt my hostility. She ended up apologizing to me about her loss of temper. I wanted to say, "Were your parents geese? Hissing and stretching your neck like that?" and, "What is prayer for, anyway, if not to use in everyday life, you idiot."

She moved out to marry again. He was a member of her church. Again the African-American safari came and carried her belongings out on their shoulders in trek style. Before she moved away, she told me with pride that she had been a precocious, promiscuous girl and started having sex from the age of fourteen, and "probably have slept with a thousand or more men in my life." Her overweight smile was toothy and cheeky like Bugs Bunny. On her dresser sat an early photo of her before the weight. A starlet on the scale of Sue Lyons in *Lolita*. But many years had passed since then. I wondered if she knew it. Men were still asking her to marry them. She grinned, announcing her marriage proposal.

I saw her from a distance limping down the street during her lunch break six months later, her foot in a cast. I wondered if she'd kicked somebody or gone through some violence to herself. I'd heard that her marriage hadn't lasted.

Ursula, Who Was Hard to Bear

I had a woman who, in her words, "worked for the University, " take the studio out back. She was in a hurry to move in. I checked her references, or should have— sometimes I'm lax and go with an instinct. This woman was my age, had been a homeowner herself in L.A. She had a daughter going off to some fancy East Coast ivy league school which she was so proud of that she kept mentioning it. Also, she was telling me she had money to send her there, which meant she could pay her rent. I took her deposit and first month's rent and she hired my son, who was visiting and had a truck, to move her in. The first load smelled of cat spray. I began humming that song, "With My Eyes Wide Open I'm Dreaming…" That was the red flag I chose not to notice. In fact, I went into a kind of victim state of politeness. I saw the rust-colored stains of cat piss all around the edges of her big stale mattress and still didn't say, "Whoa." Later I would say, "Oh, woe is me." I had the money in my hand and like the monkey with its hand in a jar of candy, couldn't let go. To let go meant I would lose another couple of week's rent and have to go through all the screening, spending plenty on running the ad again. I went limp-wristed and weak in the knees and let her happen to me.

She would cost me two thousand dollars worth of Service Master scent detection, citrus deodorizing, carpet-replacing, emotionally demoralizing, repainting loss. That last month, she would keep her door shut tight and blinds down, and refuse to pay her rent so that she could use up her deposit and move out and leave me with the expense of cleaning up after her. I gave her a three-day pay or quit, and then a 30-day notice to vacate the premises. She set her jowls in a smirk and began to convince herself that I ran a slumlord property, that the studio was a dump, and that she was more than justified to treat me this way. When I appeared with the signed rental agreement to remind her that I had a legal right to expect the rent, she let it drop in the doorway, saying that it was a farce. She said that had kept her from having a love life because of my rule of one overnighter a week and that she could take me to court for it. I looked at this obese dyed red-haired woman. How pitiful the human gets when it wants not to pay for consequences of its actions. Her two uncut male cats had ruined the cute little studio that had been freshly painted and carpeted when she moved in. A decent landlady I was, wanting to charge a fair rent for a decently kept place. I knew why landladies had a reputation for being hags, bags, mercenary, penurious creeps. I was now that in her book. She hated me because she wanted to cheat me and had to see me in a bad light. She said she knew everything about me with such a leer I wondered what that deep, dark thing could be. She went to each of the other tenants and told them in turn that they, themselves, was the only sane ones on the property and her only source of comfort since she moved in. Each in turn, came to me and reported this with humor. They had had nothing to do with her, in fact. My tenants usually did not get together. They were like me, solitude seekers, and would not have sought out the attention of this middle-aged ex-homeowner who divorced her husband because he was a gambler and gambled away their "fortune."

This woman stayed about a year and liked to sit around and talk with anyone who would oblige. She caught me several times, and I even served her coffee and chips and dip under the new patio table and umbrella. She shared her life ever so slightly with me, and asked gobs of questions about mine. I was pretty open, since she was the same age and had been through a divorce, too. Woman to woman. Looking back, I see that she didn't want to give me any information about her that might let me trace her and collect damages owed. She planned to damage the property and leave in a huff.

After she was out, I did what I should have done in the beginning but didn't have the information for then. I called her former landlady and found that she had destroyed that apartment, too. Cat piss. We talked, half dumbfounded over this woman going from place to place, costing landladies thousands of dollars just so she could "not have to do that to my cat." She was against castrating the beasts. Perhaps that's why her husband left. He couldn't stand the smell. When I did my walk-throughs every couple of months, I pointed out the smell. She claimed that she couldn't smell it. Because of her weight, she took long baths every afternoon, floating in the tub like a walrus, no doubt, to get the weight off her flipper-angled feet.

I won in court, taking in a piece of paper she had left behind that had a bright yellow spray of cat piss on it for the judge to smell. I captioned it with an arrow. He smiled, from his platform, juggling my paperwork, and said he would decline taking a whiff. I won. I still hold the judgment agaist her, but, unfortunately the deposit was for the same amount as the rent. "Five hundred and five hundred to move in, not to be used as a last."

I sent the marshal out to her bank (a bank statement she'd left in the garbage revealed which one), and he could collect only a hundred dollars. She'd cleaned out her account in a hurry, not showing up for court and knowing I'd win by her absence. What would she have to tell the judge in her behalf anyway?

She was all bluff. When she'd moved in, she praised the beauty of the place, etc. Nevertheless, her nasty comments were meant to jab, and they did. Once a tenant cheats you, moves out mad to justify it, it leaves a bad taste in your mouth, especially if the smell is so bad you can actually taste it. But, did I learn anything? Probably not. A landlady can never predict that her next choice won't be just as bad.

The Two Zoo Keepers
or
Sammy and Pammy

Sammy called first. Said he was tired of working his rent out by tending to a dozen cages of birds every night for a couple who raised cockatoos to sell. They lived way back in the hills somewhere and let him live in a trailer by the house. I was delighted. He sounded like a hard worker, had a good job tending animals at the zoo, a soft-spoken voice, and wanted a room he could come home to, to relax in. He came out and looked at the place and wanted it at the end of the month. He put down a deposit for me to hold it for him and I was perfectly happy with the deal.

Then the phone rang and it was Pam. She was a zoo keeper, too. I told her I'd had a call by another zoo keeper, and she laughed. Yes, she knew him. He was very nice. They had different responsibilities. She herself specialized in elephants. They were artificially inseminating a female elephant at the moment. She worked long hours because most work had to go on out of the public view. She just needed a room to come home to to rest so she could go back to work. At the present she was taking care of cagefuls of birds for some breeder on a ranch, and just wanted to lessen her load. And she had a cat a friend had given her for her birthday. She'd had it only a few months. Yes, that would be alright. I made a second room available;

and couldn't believe my good luck. These two tenants would be a step up from the barely employed that I usually took in.

And they were. They turned out to be ideal tenants, hardly ever there, paid their rent on time without looking resentful or pitiful, and had no attitude to put up with. Usually with one stroke of the pen a tenant's gratitude to be accepted, changes to attitude as soon as they know they're in. Sammy and Pammy worked long hours, came home, made their dinner, went to their rooms to eat it and watch TV. They were each neat, cleaning up the kichen and their shared bathroom, had their own throw rugs and bought their own cleaning agents. Each was very organized, right down to their mementos, dusted and placed on the shelving just so. Their posters tacked to the wall were of endanged species, artifacts were from travel to a few exotic places to study animals, ordinary bedspreads, clothes, clean and tidy, not expensive. They turned out to be two of the most sensible, sensitive, polite, and trouble-free tenants I'd ever had.

They were each on their way into successful futures, had no baggage from the past that interfered in their relationships with people, and generally created a decent and friendly atmosphere around the place. They were, in fact, boring in their lack of neurosis, as far as tenants go. The dynamic of failure was missing. They spent themselves at work and had no urge to create havoc at home. Home was a refuge, a place to rest, a haven away from wild animals.

I think they considered me just another primate, and kindness to animals was their profession. Just as I was kicking back and enjoying the absence of problems they gave notice. That was the only adrenaline rush I got over their tenancy, to learn that their stay would turn out to be short. Each transferred out too soon. I found myself telling people that the good ones always leave. In reality, being a zoo keeper is an ever moving process of opportunities to step up into higher and higher positions, I learned. Pammy went off to a position in San Diego which she'd applied for before she moved in. She had a degree in zoo keeping. Sammy had experience and no formal degree. He was offered a position in Africa at about the same time Pammy left for San Diego. Sammy has stayed in touch over the few years, keeping me posted as to conditions in Africa, a place I've always wanted to go. He married there, a white South African, and wrote asking if I had any rentals available should he come show his new bride Santa Barbara. I was so touched by this that I called him and said that I would make room.

A friendship with an ex-tenant is a funny business. You are no longer in a business relationship, so it frees you up to add a little animation to your conversation. As a landlady, you always have to watch yourself. You always have to draw the line. But, once a good tenant moves out and wants to keep in touch, and money is not an issue anymore, you can reveal your real self up to a point. The only inhibitor is reflecting back and checking to see if you are full of contradictions. Just because you are outside the role of landlady, doesn't mean you sit around and smoke a joint, and get raucous, when you had a strict rule of conduct when they lived under your roof. You don't suddenly let down your hair, and shock them by revealing that the whole thing was a sham. No! You simply stay who you are, if, indeed, you didn't put on some false front, and enjoy the person they are also willing to reveal now that their role of tenant is over. That role is also one of some restraint, certain formality, and keeping their real one hidden up to a point. Becoming an ex-landlady can be a very pleasant experience depending on your relationship with the tenant during his occupancy in your house. And this was a new experience for me. Otherwise, I hated running into ex-tenants. And, they didn't especially like greeting me on the street either.

The only incident with these two model tenants was when Pammy's cat disappeared. She was distraught, put signs on all the telephone poles and hoped someone would find it and return it to her. She believed it had headed back for the ranch. I found it dead by the side of the road on one of my runs, and never had the heart to tell her. Yes, it was headed in the direction of the ranch she'd moved from.

Their mail still comes to my house once in a while, as does mail for ex-tenants from years ago. The change of address procedure at the Post Office leaves much to be desired. I've written Please Forward dozens of times as a landlady. It's part of the duties.

Pammy's mother came to visit while she lived here. I found a young pretty woman reading a book in the living room one day, who introduced herself as the mother. I was surprised. From Minnesota, a cold climate complexion, slender, and as sweet and smart as her daughter. She watched me make carrot juice in my juicer that afternoon and asked, "Can't you just eat carrots for the same effect?" I wanted to ask her when was the last time she ate seventeen carrots in one sitting, but didn't.

Sammy's mother was in South Dakota, working, aging, having raised him by herself. I could tell by her voice the one time she called, that she was tired. Sammy carried a bit of sadness inside. He was quiet, read a lot, stayed in his room a lot, was conscientious to a fault. He never spoke of a father, only of his mother. I had to curb my curiosity so not to be rude. I had to respect the fact that he didn't want to talk about where and who he came from. I had a sense that he had left home at fourteen or so, worked here and there, loved animals and began cleaning up after them for a job, working his way up to some higher position of expertise. And I was right. I got enough out of him to know that he'd had to pull his own weight all the way along, whereas Pammy was from a whole other background. She'd been sent off to college, studied to be a zoo keeper, got her degree, took several special training years in elephants at some place in Los Angeles. She was a big pretty young woman who wore jeans, cotton shirts, had silky dark blonde hair, white straight teeth, perfect features, and blue eyes. Sammy was dark-haired, dark-eyed, slight of build, as if he's gone hungry a lot, or had barely enough of anything ever. He wore levis or khakis, cotton tee shirts, canvas shoes, and spent evenings taping animal programs on TV. He had a large collection of these tapes stacked neatly on the shelves.

www.ingramcontent.com/pod-product-compliance
Lightning Source LLC
Chambersburg PA
CBHW022124040426
42450CB00006B/844